ST. PATRICK'S CATHEDRAL

Joy Gregory

www.av2books.com

AV² provides enriched content that supplements and complements this book. Weigl's AV² books strive to create inspired learning and engage young minds in a total learning experience.

Your AV² Media Enhanced books come alive with...

Audio
Listen to sections of the book read aloud.

Key Words
Study vocabulary, and complete a matching word activity.

Go to **www.av2books.com**, and enter this book's unique code.

Video
Watch informative video clips.

Quizzes
Test your knowledge.

BOOK CODE

L424233

Embedded Weblinks
Gain additional information for research.

Slide Show
View images and captions, and prepare a presentation.

AV² by Weigl brings you media enhanced books that support active learning.

Try This!
Complete activities and hands-on experiments.

... and much, much more!

Published by AV² by Weigl
350 5th Avenue, 59th Floor
New York, NY 10118
Websites: www.av2books.com   www.weigl.com

Library of Congress Cataloging-in-Publication Data
Gregory, Joy.
St. Patrick's Cathedral / Joy Gregory.
    pages cm. -- (Houses of faith)
 Includes index.
 ISBN 978-1-4896-2610-3 (hardcover : alk. paper) -- ISBN 978-1-4896-2614-1 (softcover : alk. paper) -- ISBN 978-1-4896-2618-9 (single-user ebk.) -- ISBN 978-1-4896-2622-6 (multi-user ebk.)1. St. Patrick's Cathedral (New York, N.Y.)--Juvenile literature. 2. Cathedrals--New York (State)--New York--Juvenile literature. 3. Manhattan (New York, N.Y.)--Buildings, structures, etc.--Juvenile literature. 4. New York (N.Y.)--Buildings, structures, etc.--Juvenile literature. I. Title.
 NA5235.N6S39 2014
 726.609747'1--dc23

                    2014038572

Printed in the United States of America in North Mankato, Minnesota
1 2 3 4 5 6 7 8 9 0 19 18 17 16 15

112014
WEP311214

Editor: Heather Kissock
Design: Mandy Christiansen

Every reasonable effort has been made to trace ownership and to obtain permission to reprint copyright material. The publishers would be pleased to have any errors or omissions brought to their attention so that they may be corrected in subsequent printings. Weigl acknowledges Getty Images, Alamy, iStockphoto, Dreamstime, and Newscom as its primary image suppliers for this title.

Contents

What Is St. Patrick's Cathedral?

Located on the island of Manhattan in New York City, St. Patrick's Cathedral is one of the best-known Roman Catholic cathedrals in the United States. The cathedral is the **seat** of the **archbishop** of New York. As such, it is the central church of New York City's Roman Catholic community.

St. Patrick's Cathedral was built to replace an older, smaller cathedral that was no longer able to meet the needs of the growing **parish**. During the 1800s, many Europeans were moving to the United States, and to New York City in particular. The archbishop of New York decided that a newer, grander cathedral would reflect the growth taking place in both the parish and the city.

When first built, St. Patrick's **spires** could be seen from 20 miles (32.2 kilometers) away. Today, they are dwarfed by the city's many skyscrapers. The cathedral remains, however, an important place of worship for New York's Roman Catholics. Over time, it has also become a popular tourist site. Many visitors to New York City come to the cathedral to marvel at its size and **architectural** beauty.

Since its construction, St. Patrick's Cathedral has played a central role in the lives of Roman Catholics in New York and the United States as a whole.

The Roman Catholic Faith

Roman Catholicism is a Christian religion. This means it is based on the teachings of Jesus Christ, a man believed to have lived more than 2,000 years ago. Followers of the Roman Catholic faith share several beliefs with other Christians. They believe that Jesus Christ was the son of God, and they read a book called the Bible for spiritual inspiration. However, Roman Catholicism has several beliefs that are unique. For instance, Roman Catholics believe that **saints** can cure illnesses and help people in need. They also believe in a place called purgatory that prepares people to enter heaven after they have died.

The Roman Catholic Church is led by the pope. Pope means **"papa," or father.**

24% of all Americans are Roman Catholic.

About **2.6 million** Catholics live in the archdiocese of New York. An archdiocese is the area cared for by an archbishop.

Roman Catholics Around the World

Latin America	483 million
Europe	277 million
Africa	177 million
Asia	137 million
North America	85 million
Oceania	9 million

A Step Back in Time

When the decision was made to build a new cathedral, the archbishop began to look for a location that would allow for a larger structure. He soon decided on a site on New York's Fifth Avenue, a part of the city that was still relatively undeveloped at the time. One of the country's top architects, James Renwick, Jr., was then hired to design the new building.

Renwick chose to create the cathedral in the Gothic Revival style. This architectural style is based on the structures of the Middle Ages. Gothic Revival buildings are known for their soaring towers, pointed arches, and steeply slanted roofs.

CONSTRUCTION TIMELINE

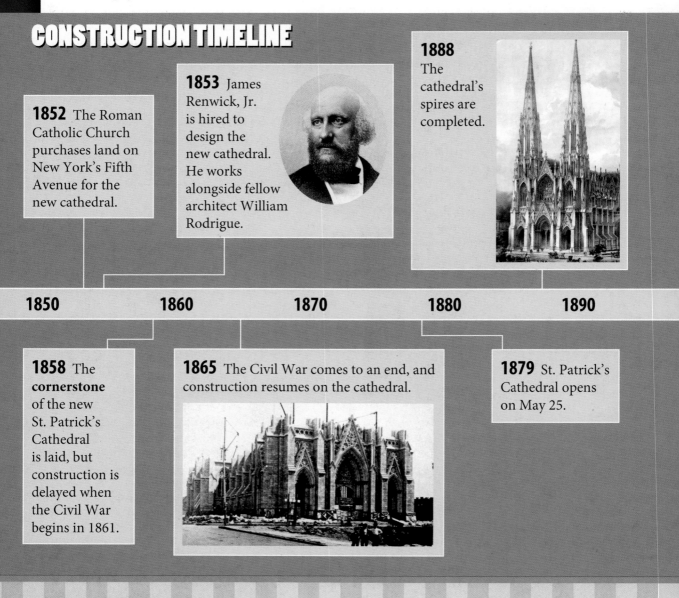

1852 The Roman Catholic Church purchases land on New York's Fifth Avenue for the new cathedral.

1853 James Renwick, Jr. is hired to design the new cathedral. He works alongside fellow architect William Rodrigue.

1888 The cathedral's spires are completed.

1850   1860   1870   1880   1890

1858 The **cornerstone** of the new St. Patrick's Cathedral is laid, but construction is delayed when the Civil War begins in 1861.

1865 The Civil War comes to an end, and construction resumes on the cathedral.

1879 St. Patrick's Cathedral opens on May 25.

The construction process was only expected to take eight years. The start of the Civil War, however, brought work on the building to a grinding halt. The cathedral took more than 20 years to complete and cost the archdiocese about $1.9 million. In the years that followed, other buildings were added to the grounds. These buildings included a **rectory**, a school, and a house for the archbishop.

The cathedral was named after Saint Patrick, the patron saint of Ireland. This was in honor of the many Irish Catholic immigrants arriving in New York in the 1800s.

1927 The first major **renovation** includes building a larger **sanctuary**. The choir gallery is also rebuilt, and new pews are added.

1976 The cathedral and associated buildings are declared a National Historic Landmark.

2012 The archdiocese announces long-term plans to maintain and preserve the cathedral for future generations.

1900   1950   1975   2000   2015

1900 Construction of the Lady Chapel begins. The chapel is completed in 1908.

1950s The Great Rose Window is installed over the west entrance.

St. Patrick's Location

Nestled between 50th and 51st Streets, St. Patrick's Fifth Avenue location is now considered prime real estate. This part of Manhattan is known as a business and entertainment hub. Fifth Avenue itself is home to some of New York's most iconic structures. It also features some of the world's best-known shopping venues.

WIDTH At its widest point, the cathedral measures 274 feet (84 meters) across.

SPIRES The spires of St. Patrick's Cathedral reach a height of 330 feet (101 m).

The cathedral is across the street from Rockefeller Center, a complex that includes television studios and commercial buildings. Saks Fifth Avenue, a luxury department store, sits across from St. Patrick's. Several other well-known buildings, including the Empire State Building, Trump Tower, Chrysler Building, Grand Central Terminal, and the United Nations Headquarters, are also within walking distance of the cathedral.

NEW YORK

New York City

Atlantic Ocean

0   125 Miles
0   125 Km

LENGTH The total length of the cathedral is 405 feet (123 m).

St. Patrick's Cathedral is an active parish church. Services are held daily at various times to meet the needs of the parishioners.

Touring the Exterior

The Gothic Revival architecture of St. Patrick's Cathedral helps the structure stand out from the skyscrapers and commercial buildings that surround it.

FAÇADE The west **façade** is the main entrance of the cathedral. The entrance consists of three doors made of solid bronze. The center door is the largest of the three. Each of the doors is decorated with sculptures of saints and other religious figures. The façade features several windows, each supported by intricate **tracery**. Most of the façade is made of Tuckahoe marble, a type of rock found in New York.

SPIRES Two spires topped with copper crosses frame the main entrance to St. Patrick's Cathedral. At roof level, the spires are four-sided structures that look like **medieval** castle towers. Above the roof line, the spires adopt an octagonal form. The north spire serves as the cathedral's bell tower. Its 19 bells ring out to announce services and ceremonies.

BUTTRESSES Each spire is supported by a massive **buttress** that extends up its side. These buttresses are topped with small spires called pinnacles. Each of the tower's buttresses has a circular stone stairway inside that leads to the organ gallery and the upper levels of the spires. A series of buttresses also run along the sides of the cathedral itself. These buttresses were built to support a stone roof that was planned for the cathedral, but never built.

Tuckahoe marble was chosen as the cathedral's main building material because of its unique light cream color.

New York's annual St. Patrick's Day parade is one of the largest parades in the world. The parade route includes a march past St. Patrick's Cathedral.

St. Patrick's roof is capped with 343 stone ornaments called finials.

One of the best views of the cathedral is found across the street near *Atlas*, a bronze sculpture located in front of Rockefeller Center.

The center doors stand 16.5 feet (5 m) high. Each door is 5.5 feet (1.7 m) wide.

Unlike the rest of the façade, the cathedral's spires are made from Cockeysville marble, which is found in Maryland.

More than
5.5 MILLION
people visit the cathedral every year.

The cathedral can seat
2,200 people.

Every year, visitors to the cathedral light **more than 1 million** prayer candles.

All together, the bells of St. Patrick's weigh more than **29,000 pounds** (13,154 kilograms).

Each of St. Patrick's bells is named after a saint.

Each of the center doors on the west façade weighs **9,200 pounds** (4,173 kg).

Inside St. Patrick's

*The interior of St. Patrick's is known for its **vaulted** ceiling and marble columns. Shaped in the form of a cross, its design pays tribute to its religious purpose.*

SANCTUARY The sanctuary lies at the front of the cathedral's **nave**. Surrounded by a large wooden screen, the sanctuary is where the cathedral's main **altar** is located. It is from here that the archbishop of New York performs mass and other ceremonies. A 57-foot (17.4-m) tall **baldachin** sits above the altar. Underneath the sanctuary is the **crypt**, where the cathedral's former archbishops are buried.

LADY CHAPEL Behind the sanctuary lies the Lady Chapel. This small chapel was not part of the original cathedral. It was built in the early 1900s to serve as a place of prayer and reflection. The chapel features a series of stained glass windows that run around its exterior walls. A statue of Our Lady of New York stands above the chapel's altar.

STAINED GLASS WINDOWS Light flows into St. Patrick's Cathedral through its many stained glass windows. Most of these windows portray saints and other religious figures. The Great Rose Window is located above the center doors of the main entrance. It features overlapping arcs that look like flower petals. The Founders' Window is located on the south **transept**. One of its panels shows St. Patrick preaching to a group of peasants. Another panel features the cathedral's architect, James Renwick, Jr.

Rows of pews fill the floor of the nave, while a series of small altars runs around its perimeter.

The Lady Chapel was built to honor Mary, the mother of Jesus Christ.

A sculpture called the *Pieta* sits just outside the Lady Chapel. Sculpted by William Ordway Partridge, it shows Mary holding the body of Jesus Christ in her arms.

Before the most recent renovation, the sanctuary contained two altars. The low altar sat in front of the high, or main, altar.

The bronze baldachin has stood over the main altar since 1942, when the sanctuary was remodeled.

For Roman Catholics, lighting candles is a form of prayer. St. Patrick's has placed candle stations throughout the cathedral for this purpose.

The cathedral's stained glass windows contain more than

2,800

stained glass panels in total.

The Great Rose Window is 27 feet (8.2 m) in diameter.

The Lady Chapel is about the same size in length and height, measuring about **57 feet (17 m)** in each direction.

St. Patrick's Cathedral has two organs. Together, these organs have more than **9,000** pipes.

More than **100,000** weddings have been performed in St. Patrick's since it opened in 1879.

Visitors cannot take pictures in the Lady Chapel.

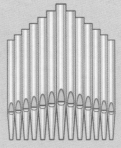

The Science behind St. Patrick's

Building a strong and sturdy structure that will stand the test of time requires a solid understanding of scientific principles. Architects and other members of the building team must know which materials and techniques will support the building's design. St. Patrick's builders selected the materials and design features that they believed would create a long-lasting structure, as well as represent its religious intent.

THE PROPERTIES OF MARBLE St. Patrick's walls, towers, columns, and other key structures are made of marble. Much of this marble was **quarried** in New York and Massachusetts. However, the Lady Chapel was built using marble from Vermont. Marble was chosen because it is a soft rock. The measurement of hardness scale (Mohs) determines the hardness of a stone based on how easily it can be scratched by grit or hard objects. The scale rates rocks from one to ten, with ten being the hardest form of rock. Marble is a three out of ten on this scale. This means it can be easily cut and shaped, allowing builders to create structures that have intricate designs sculpted into them.

POINTED ARCHES One of the main features of Gothic Revival architecture is the use of pointed arches. Arches have been used in architecture since 300 BC. They are able to support heavy weight because they change the direction of the weight's force. Instead of pressing downward, the force of the weight is pushed outward. This spreads the weight of the structure evenly across a larger area. Pointed arches allow a building to have greater height than rounded arches. In the case of St. Patrick's, pointed arches have been used to create the series of **rib vaults** that form the ceiling. The rib vaults distribute the weight of the ceiling more evenly, putting less stress on the cathedral's walls.

CASTING BRONZE Several of St. Patrick's decorative features, including the front doors and the baldachin, are made of bronze. Bronze is an alloy of copper. That means it is made of two or more metals. Typical metals used to make bronze include copper, zinc, and tin. The act of turning a copper alloy into a decorative piece of metal is called casting. To begin, the artist carves the piece out of wax. The carving is then covered in a material that hardens over the wax. The wax and covering are heated. The wax melts away, but the covering stays. The copper alloy is then heated to melt the metal. The melted metal, or bronze, is poured into the empty space where the wax used to be. After the bronze cools, the covering is broken, and the statue remains.

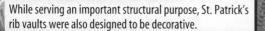

While serving an important structural purpose, St. Patrick's rib vaults were also designed to be decorative.

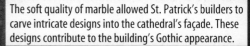

The soft quality of marble allowed St. Patrick's builders to carve intricate designs into the cathedral's façade. These designs contribute to the building's Gothic appearance.

A series of arches extend along the outside walls of the cathedral. These arches support the triforium, which is a second-story gallery that runs around the interior walls of the building.

St. Patrick's bronze baldachin features sculptures of important religious figures, including several saints and prophets.

St. Patrick's Builders

St. Patrick's Cathedral was designed by architects, built by construction workers, and decorated by artists who worked with wood, bronze, glass, and stone. Some of these people were involved in the initial construction. Others worked on expanding the structure into what it is today.

James Renwick, Jr. James Renwick, Jr. was born in New York in 1818. At the age of 12, Renwick began studying **engineering** at Columbia University, graduating with a master's degree in 1839. He then went to work as a structural engineer for a railway company. Renwick had no formal training in architecture, but he did have a keen interest in building design. After winning a competition for his design of a church, Renwick began his career as an architect. Besides designing several U.S. churches, he was also the architect of the original Smithsonian Institution Building in Washington, DC, known as "The Castle." St. Patrick's Cathedral, however, remains his best-known work.

William Rodrigue William Rodrigue was born in Philadelphia, Pennsylvania, in 1800. An interest in art led him to study in Paris, France. When he returned to the United States in 1823, he began working for a Philadelphia architectural firm. He left the company in 1830 to work independently. Besides St. Patrick's Cathedral, Rodrigue is also credited with designing Philadelphia's Church of Saint John, as well as the Church of St. Francis Xavier, in New York.

The baldachin was added to the cathedral's sanctuary as part of Charles Donagh Maginnis's remodeling. Its installation was an effort to make this part of the cathedral more Gothic in style.

Charles T. Mathews

Charles T. Mathews was an American who was born in 1863 in Paris, France. Receiving his early schooling in France, he later moved to the United States to study at both Columbia and Yale Universities. He then returned to France to receive his architectural training. In 1900, Mathews submitted his design for St. Patrick's Lady Chapel. Construction of the chapel began later that year. He was also responsible for the remodeling of New York's Church of the Holy Trinity. Over the years, Mathews became known for his writings on art and architecture.

Charles Donagh Maginnis

Charles Donagh Maginnis was responsible for redesigning St. Patrick's main altar. Born in Londonderry, Ireland, Maginnis studied in Dublin before joining an architectural firm in Boston, Massachusetts, in 1888. He eventually left the firm to form his own company. Maginnis is sometimes referred to as the "Father of Gothic Revival Architecture in America." He was responsible for designing the campus of Boston College, as well as several well-known American churches and cathedrals.

Charles Jay Connick

St. Patrick's Great Rose Window showcases the artistry of Charles Jay Connick. Known as one of America's greatest stained glass artists, Connick was born in Springboro, Pennsylvania, in 1875. After receiving his art training in Pittsburgh, he moved to Boston, where he opened his own art studio. Connick was a key figure in the Gothic Revival movement in the United States. His windows can be seen in many of the country's best-known Gothic Revival churches.

Similar Structures around the World

Gothic Revival architecture began in the 18th century. It is sometimes referred to as "neo" or "new" Gothic. The first Gothic Revival buildings were private homes in rural areas. By the early 1800s, the style was popular with churches and government buildings in various parts of the world.

Washington National Cathedral

BUILT: 1907–1990
LOCATION: Washington, DC, United States
DESIGN: George Frederick Bodley, Henry Vaughan, Philip H. Frohman, and Frohman, Robb & Little
DESCRIPTION: Sometimes called America's longest construction project, Washington National Cathedral is a spiritual gathering place for people of all faiths. The cathedral's first stone was taken from a field near Bethlehem. However, the building is mostly made of Indiana limestone. The cathedral's Gothic Revival features include three towers, several stained glass windows, and **flying buttresses**.

The Washington National Cathedral is the second largest cathedral in the United States and the sixth largest cathedral in the world.

Votive Church

BUILT: 1856–1879
LOCATION: Vienna, Austria
DESIGN: Heinrich von Ferstel
DESCRIPTION: Vienna's Votive Church was built to give thanks for saving the life of Emperor Franz Joseph after an assassination attempt. Its two towers soar 325 feet (99 m) above the church's rose window and main entrance. A smaller spire rises from the church transept. The interior has two aisles, which separate the smaller chapels from the main part of the nave. The main altar is made of marble that has been decorated with glass **mosaics**. The altar is supported by six columns.

The Votive Church was one of the first churches to be built in the Gothic Revival style.

Cathedral of La Plata

Approximately 12 million bricks line the Cathedral of La Plata's walls.

BUILT: 1884–1902
LOCATION: La Plata, Argentina
DESIGN: Ernesto Meyer, Pedro Benoit
DESCRIPTION: The Cathedral of La Plata is one of the largest cathedrals in the Americas. Made mainly of brick and copper, the cathedral's design features eight towers, each of a different height. The two largest towers are said to represent Jesus Christ and Mary. The interior of the cathedral is made up of five naves. Besides the cathedral's main altar, there are also three secondary altars. Stained glass windows run along the walls, allowing light to enter the cathedral. Each window contains a scene from the Bible.

Issues Facing St. Patrick's

St. Patrick's has stood in central Manhattan for more than 100 years. As the city has grown and changed, the cathedral has been impacted in several ways. The heavy use by both worshippers and tourists, along with exposure to the environment, have caused damage to the structure, inside and out.

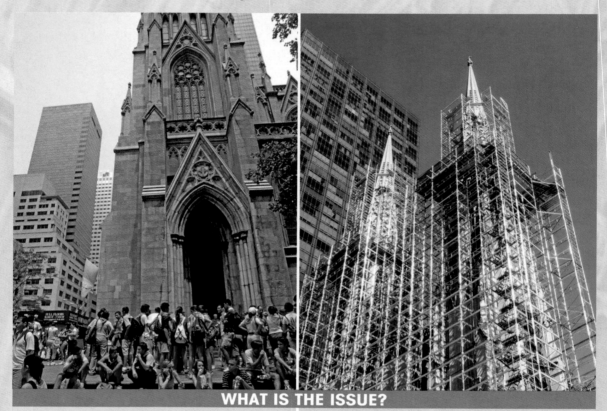

WHAT IS THE ISSUE?

The large number of visitors has caused wear and tear in high-volume areas.

Over the years, the building has been constantly exposed to environmental conditions that include a harsh climate and industrial pollution.

EFFECTS

The main doors, wooden pews, and tiled floors have lost their finish.

With constant exposure to the elements, layers of grime have accumulated on the building.

ACTION TAKEN

A major interior and exterior renovation project was launched in 2012. Part of the renovation includes refinishing areas that have lost their luster through overuse.

A major cleaning of the interior and exterior stonework is expected to be completed in 2015. The accumulated grime is being removed, restoring the stone to its original color. Cracks in the stonework are also being repaired as part of this process.

Create a Cast Sculpture

Bronze is just one material that can be cast into sculptures and other art forms. Follow the instructions below to cast an artistic masterpiece of your own.

Materials

- foam plate
- ballpoint pen
- plaster of Paris
- craft stick or wooden spoon
- mixing bowl
- bronze craft paint
- paintbrush

Instructions

1. Use the ballpoint pen to draw a pattern or picture on the foam plate. Press the pen hard enough to make an imprint of the design, but do not poke it through the plate.

2. Mix the plaster of Paris according to the directions on the package. This will involve pouring water into the plaster and stirring it with the wooden spoon or craft stick. The plaster is ready when it looks like pancake batter.

3. Pour the plaster of Paris into your foam plate.

4. Let it sit overnight.

5. Remove the hardened plaster, or sculpture, from the plate. It should come off the plate in one piece.

6. Paint the sculpture to make it look like a piece of bronze art.

St. Patrick's Cathedral Quiz

Q Which architectural style was used to design the cathedral?

A Gothic Revival

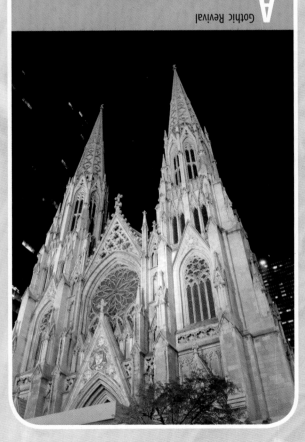

Q How many people visit St. Patrick's Cathedral every year?

A More than 5.5 million

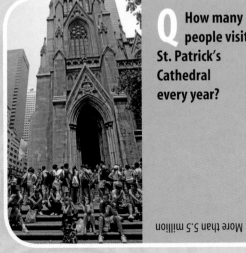

Q Who designed the Great Rose Window?

A Charles Jay Connick

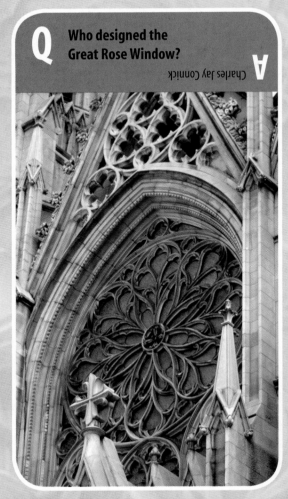

Q What type of marble was used to create much of St. Patrick's façade?

A Tuckahoe marble

Key Words

altar: an elevated structure where religious ceremonies are performed

archbishop: a senior member of the church

architectural: related to the design of buildings

baldachin: a ceremonial canopy placed over an altar

buttress: a support that projects out from a wall

cornerstone: a foundation stone

crypt: an underground room below a church used for burials

engineering: applying scientific principles to the design of structures

façade: the principal front of a building

flying buttresses: arched buttresses extended from a wall to a pier outside the building

medieval: related to the Middle Ages of 500 AD to about 1500 AD

mosaics: designs made up of tiny colored tiles

nave: the central space in a church where the congregation sits

parish: an area with its own church and priest

quarried: the act of digging stone from a pit

rectory: a house where a priest lives

renovation: changes or repairs to a building

rib vaults: a framework of several pointed arches and intersecting stone ribs that support a vaulted ceiling

saints: people who have been officially recognized as holy by the Church

sanctuary: the room in a church where a religious service is held

seat: a center of authority

spires: structures that taper to a point at the top

tracery: delicate interlacing decor, such as carving, found in the upper part of Gothic Revival windows

transept: the part of a church that crosses the nave at right angles

vaulted: arched to form a ceiling or roof

Index

Log on to www.av2books.com

AV² by Weigl brings you media enhanced books that support active learning. Go to www.av2books.com, and enter the special code found on page 2 of this book. You will gain access to enriched and enhanced content that supplements and complements this book. Content includes video, audio, weblinks, quizzes, a slide show, and activities.

AV² Online Navigation

Book Pages
AV² pages directly correspond to pages in the book.

Audio
Listen to sections of the book read aloud.

Key Words
Study vocabulary, and complete a matching word activity.

Quizzes
Test your knowledge.

Slide Show
View images and captions, and prepare a presentation.

Video
Watch informative video clips.

Embedded Weblinks
Gain additional information for research.

Try This!
Complete activities and hands-on experiments.

AV² was built to bridge the gap between print and digital. We encourage you to tell us what you like and what you want to see in the future.

Sign up to be an AV² Ambassador at www.av2books.com/ambassador.